how to spear sleep

ALSO BY NATHAN SHEPHERDSON

the day the artists stood still (volume one)
clouds in another's blood
Apples with Human Skin
what marian drew never told me about light
Sweeping the Light Back into the Mirror

Nathan Shepherdson

how to
spear sleep

Shearsman Books

First published in the United Kingdom in 2021 by
Shearsman Books Ltd
PO Box 4239
Swindon
SN3 9FN

Shearsman Books Ltd Registered Office
30–31 St. James Place, Mangotsfield, Bristol BS16 9JB
(this address not for correspondence)

www.shearsman.com

ISBN 978-1-84861-741-4

For Felicity Plunkett

Contents

253°

for three days
   i have been unable
   to injure the silence
in what you ask

i kick away the dust
and realise we're all walking
on the hypnotist's lips

131°

this piece of string
between our teeth

sags

as we near the middle
and shake hands

33°

the clouds i banked
in the eyes of the donkey
i would withdraw
as the price for this animal
to swap its head for mine
    to pay for the decision
        as stubborn as a corner to a square
          opened out inside its own belief

270°

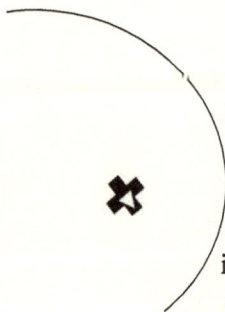

the door handle
  calls him by his proper name

turns one hand
into the loneliest of saints

tells the other hand
not to pray for him at all

349°

in turn

you position your foot
on my forearm

heel tucked into elbow
wrist boundary set to toe

then i place my foot
on your forearm

wrist boundary set to toe
    heel tucked into elbow

        but

            for the different ages
        in our blood
            under pressure of the sole

        our fit is perfect

281°

the breeze → →   →
moves your mother's hair to speech
  as we sit outside for breakfast
    marmalade on sourdough
      she sips coffee in schwarzlot detail
        resettles orbit of cup to saucer
          with unmistakable crockery kiss

      after breakfast
    i undo my shirt
  and crudely print last night's poem
off my sun-glazed stomach
onto a pale blue serviette

39°

waiting for the sun
to burn off the fog
around your head

mist-small waves
propel forward
under-roll back
in treble clef curls
exhaled →
by your blinking eyes

300°

you are not the same as death

i'm certainly not the same as life

on the other side of this sentence
they're arranging our throats
as an intersection
to allow skin
to grow over
the traffic of words

we swallow

67°

a single almond
on the floor
is a storehouse
for gravity

not looked at
it stands on its tip
a static ballet
dreaming its tiny monument
to cyanide ←

objects
that obey their shadows
are locked
in a cry for help

it's our limbs
they will sweep away
in the morning

277°

the train
counts its passengers

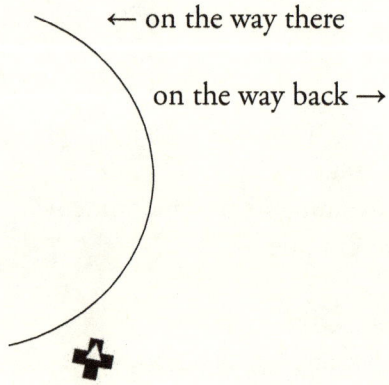

← on the way there

on the way back →

230°

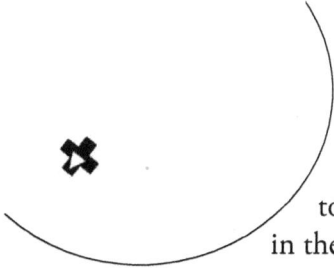

uncannily waiting
for a nonfuture
to compress diamonds
in the shape of our heads

248°

your grandma
is not in the house
she refuses to leave

✥ uniforms unfilled with bodies
march through her memory

122°

not knowing
i answered you to a lie
not even calling you an animal
but a smattering of words
    limping under the weight of this page
      is every darkness stuffed to perfect fruit
        that will taste the lanolin fact
         of my action

        you are the third object
        not as mute as the other two
      of which you carry the second
    and i hold the first
as we ascend the secret
in this geology
that will also betray you

183°

it's more productive
to tie a knot in the shovel
than dig a grave

i comb your thoughts
     with my hair

        detonate the owl
        with our last night

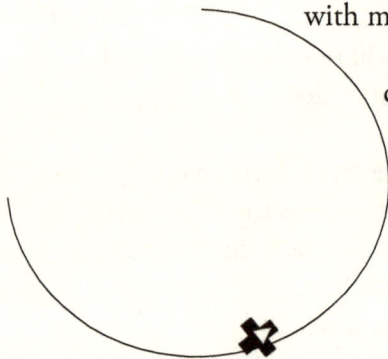

141°

in this tank
our shadows are preserved in brine

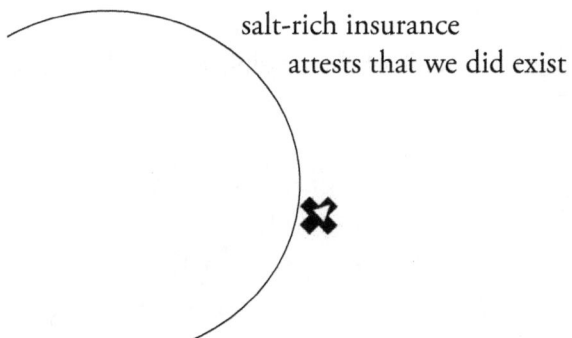

salt-rich insurance
attests that we did exist

12°

walking three foot above the ground

air scoffs at his surprise

suicide of the possible allows all possibility

55°

un/able

to lift the glass dome
covering the matchbook
taken from the dictator's pocket
at my recital

if/able

to lift the glass dome
over the matchbook
stolen from the dictator's pocket
at your recital

   /

i would rub spit
into the monolimb of each match
     transform them into worms
        that would burrow through the earth
       to extinguish the magma
      in these poisonous hearts

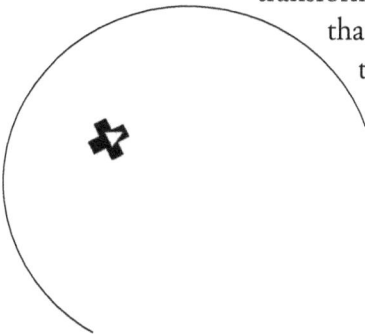

95°

i knew skin
promised more than life
in the way it lies

why are these words
so easy to pronounce

nothing will be remembered
when we remember
its name

302°

despite being damaged

if i turn this cameo ring
holding your grandad's portrait

(under)

   slowly
    clench my fist
     into a bone bud

    you fall asleep
    within seconds

(within)

(seconds)

hear what i can't say

315°

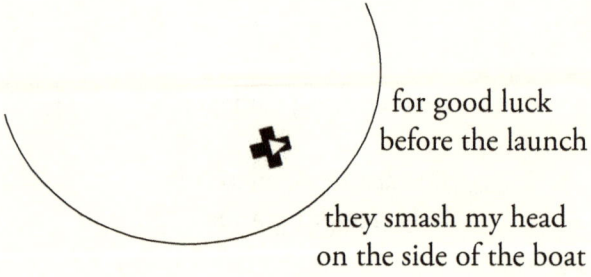

for good luck
before the launch

they smash my head
on the side of the boat

150°

(unfortunately)

you'll need to be a zookeeper
when academics
start swinging from my ribs

(like thesis monkeys)

67°

.shot/reply/shhot.

.shot/replyy/shott/repply.

our language
would normally add tension
to the net

but today
we ignore words
for movement

rally thought to reflex

stick our usual masks
to mirror shapes in hand
and share the celluloid solo
of this two-bat jazz
pumping a corollary of laughter
around our atomised brains
at no expense to the management

all this/   /
until strong schnapps
        and a roast leg of lamb
            on a different table
            comes with the advice
             our table tennis is over

             the net posts
            a witty memorial
            to our absence

we put the ball
back in Orion's belt

the best tailors work at night
and our bodies offer them no exception

later i return
to the person
you fear in me

pulling down my lower lids
to reveal gravity's duplex accommodation

in the reminiscence
you are yet to write
you perceptively mention →
'the sadness he knew how to spread'

359°

would i shit the world
into my son's hand

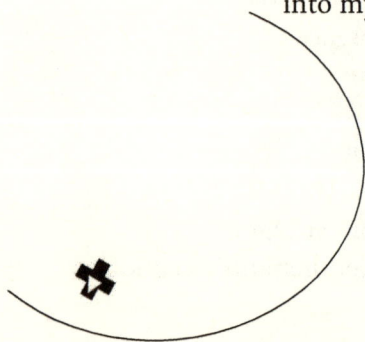

no.

7°

i did not salt the potatoes

to again avoid seeing
how the crystals sweat
        their colonising power
            across the dirt-pink skin
                of these tuber moons

                my teeth quote themselves

218°

in the index of apologies
my finger fails
    to locate your name

        the simplest philosophy
          is to piss on a question
          when it's dead

       until it's dead
      i fail to locate
    my finger

or piss on a question
in your name

288°

it's standard practice
to replace our lungs
with fine leather gloves
        so they can laugh at us
            while we take
                our ten last breaths

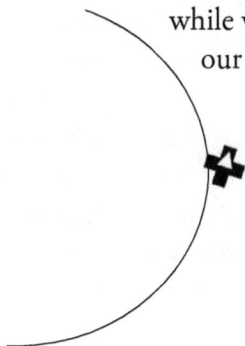

20°

i can't bend my elbows
because of the nails
  through my hands

    you'll notice
    it's my blood
     on the doorpost
     as you pass over
     → the threshold
      into the illusion
      that you passed over
    → the threshold
for a different path

silence waits for your ears
to slide down over your nipples
to listen to the two hearts
they know you have

126°

i want you
to carry my thumbs
in your wallet

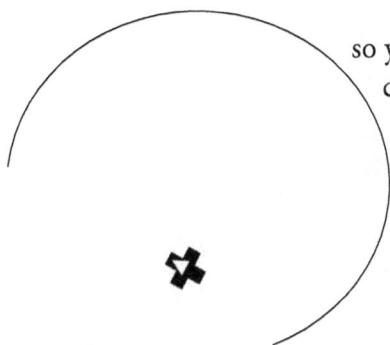

        so your best memories
          can use them as skis
            to escape the avalanche

155°

i suck on the end of each word
    before threading them
        through a hole in your tongue

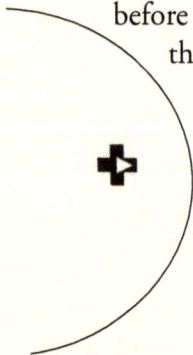

220°

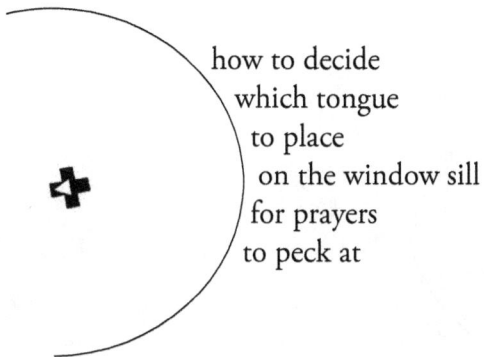

how to decide
which tongue
to place
on the window sill
for prayers
to peck at

113°

you are the final language
from which i am

removed

from which i

am

↓

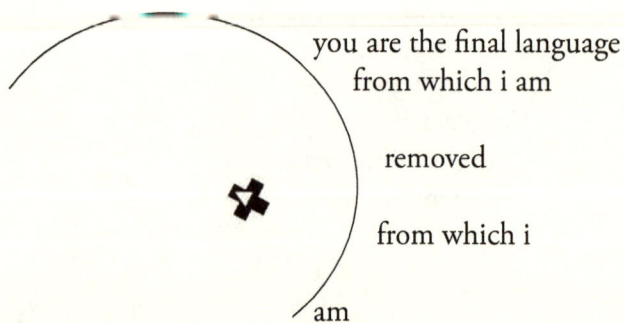

my neck
an umbrella stand
half full of rain
that never fell

248°

when i am
in the cave with your mother
a cave full of years ←
a cave full of the absence of years →
when our flesh has bought tickets
to an odourless land
you will have all i have

and i have nothing
but a handful of seeds
to grow faces instead of corn
in fertile definition

you will water these faces

16°

i will possess my enemies
after they have killed me

i draw still outlines
around their bodies
but not they mine
    as never was i seen
       to copy their lives
          into another's words
        or even speak words
        i did not misuse
         deep inside the eulogy
    of any moment (   )

   i rub my fluid
into the hinges
of their gate

and when they open my name
they open their skulls
to consumption

264°

winching open the finger ends
to reveal cigar bright/white projectors
that transmit atomic plankton
into our eyes as the light
from a billion untrammelled stars

71°

twice the age of my death
when his son is born

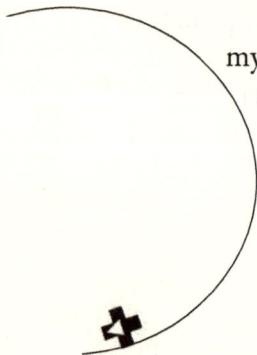

my son ←
   soaking in words
     until blood whispers its colour
     under your water

91°

my writing hand
can be set alight
without pain

on the condition
i use its flame
to burn other flesh

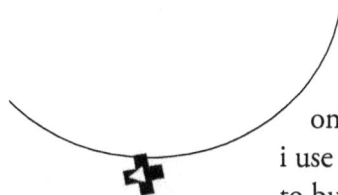

325°

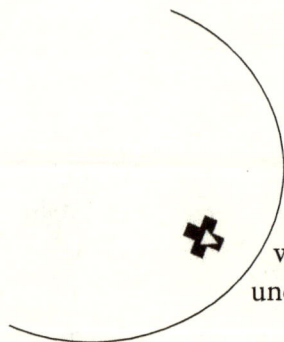

the dew
on your eyelash
will not evaporate
under the sun

unless

i let the sun
come up

158°

with a knife & fork
he's cutting up words
on his leg

separating the syllables
into fat & protein

trilobites breed in his soul

138°

line funnel with skin

pour in liquid touch

remove skin from funnel

all liquid is vanished

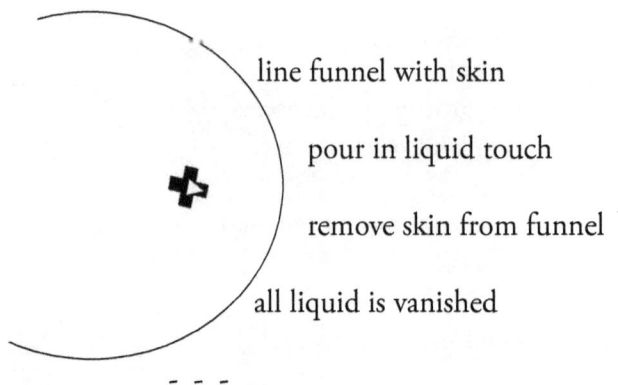

your body is sung through a porthole

151°

wasps have built a nest under my chin

stubby mud fingers
that grip my pores
with an architectural enzyme

    unconscious pressure from the tongue
      makes them bob like capsules
        on an inverted sea

95°

or the time
you rinsed undissolved organs
under the kitchen tap
your back to me
telling me to shut my eyes
you turn slowly
    and place them in my hands
      one by one
        asking me to guess
        which is which

4°

pulling a roast capsicum
out of the oven
on a Meissen plate

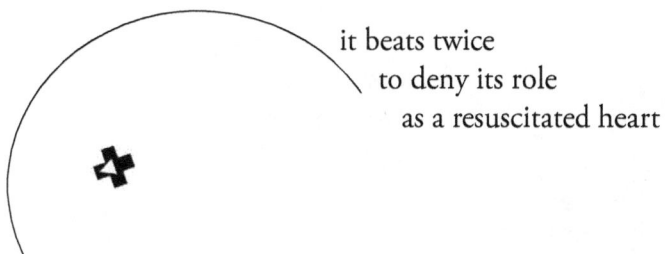

   it beats twice
     to deny its role
        as a resuscitated heart

69°

for some reason
a world would skin itself
to hang itself
as fresh meat
in the shop window
and wait for itself
as its own customer

the skin
impossible to buy
until the body is eaten

177°

as safe as a rabbit
down a hole
dusting its nose
over cross-section circles
cut to the barrel of a gun

the trigger the one comma
to pause death

Dürer pulls on his ear

155°

i'm sorry to raise my voice

but:

doES ANybody kNow
THE PHoNE NUmbEr
of THiS PAgE

:

my SoN
iS TrAPPEd iNSidE
& i doN'T kNow How
    To rEACH Him

            :

        my son
      is trapped inside
    & i don't know how
    i put him there

:

44°

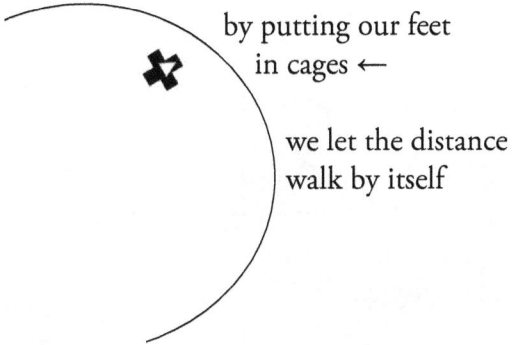

by putting our feet
in cages ←

we let the distance
walk by itself

211°

✛ leading up to this word

i fell back into space

self-digested the full stops
from a year's worth of sentences
now under the pliable expertise
of a coroner's toothpick

106°

it takes skill
to trim each match
to correct length and chamfer
to use them as vertical jacks
to hold the teeth apart
upper & lower
to repel the upward gravity
in the lower jaw
too comfortable in its own desire
to close

(↑)
(↓)

we enact this ritual
inside the mouth of the other
making sure the phosphorous heads
press under the upper teeth
so their dipped red crumbles
to accumulate a tideline
along our unignited lower lip

this is when ←
true communication occurs

our tongues unable to touch
the roofs in our mouths
can only throw an echo
to hunt spastic sounds

across our corrugated ears
that do not understand
but nonetheless believe
themselves the best luggage
covered in our identical skin

this game
is not as isolated
as the two people
who play it
to arrive at one thought

in one thought two dice
in port & starboard colours
    continually shake a cube face
       to a number which tells us
        via left & right mouth
         counted from a wisdom tooth
         forward to a first match
        removed followed by another
       dice drum a handless table
      until a new other is the first sign
    these last matches will bend
 to trip the pine scaffold
into warm saliva rapids
that again carry flattened bodies
to our isthmus tongues
revived as transplant language
bitten off at the waist
jaws finally compress their victim
inside the mouth of the other
match stakes lance the gums
to leave our unusual bloods
unsucked on a shattered timber teat

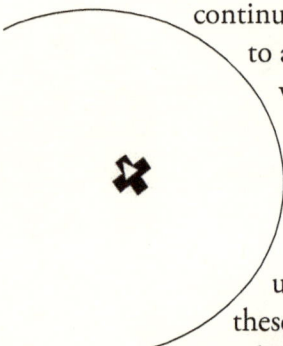

(↓)
(↑)

this game
is as isolated
as the two people
who did not play it
to arrive at one thought
they never had

we win
the displaced either
narrow to a helm
are boats always sunk
in our veins
flares gather
to remain unseen
ignited
on our upper lip

16°

i measure my head
until it's not there

          mimic the fool
            who breathes light
             into a blind sea

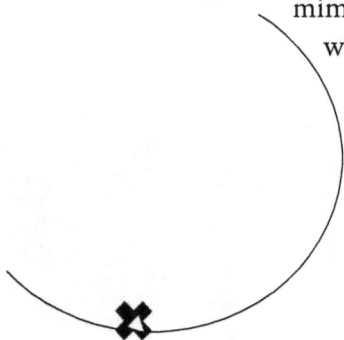

98°

still

inside this line
marking ultimate obedience

i see tears
in my son's eyes
become black crystals

300°

naked

in the same room
in separate mirrors
glued back to back

we shook death from its own clothes

did we shake death from our own

225°

with jute fibres i bind your last form

knees into chest
hands behind back

deep marks
a crosshatch of horizons

our hearts tidy four rooms with fear

your trust equal to all description

trees have already sacrificed their limbs

59°

welcome to the genre of crucifiction

in this economy of means
even the jokes are poor

save yourself
for the lightning
to conduct you
in one cruel note

126°

with a fresh set of prints
either side of our window
watching touch-contours loosen
to a jumble of light-lived marks
about to reconvene as phrase queues
unaided into microcalligraphic states
with statements like:

.guilt sucks the toe of a question mark.

.bees evolve the polar traits of a magnet.

.does murder sleep in these hands.

.their brains a praline mixture wrapped in bone.

39°

the white cymbidium headdress
your mother must also wear
before the trial
of our conversation

begins

83°

this white arc of garden furniture
supports my son as a three year old

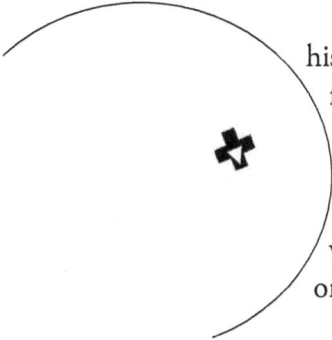

his right arm
feather-pressed to a grateful cheek

my left hand
points out a line on his playsuit
where i should write more words
on his chest

my watch refuses to look at me

the other chair turns its back

my legs crossed like two millennia

338°

this is the last time
he'll tie his shoelaces

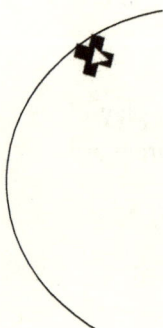

↔

when he stands up
he won't be there

88°

in parade form
why is no in the alphabet

and not yes

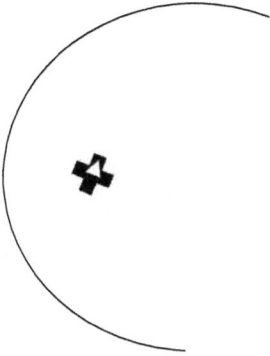

58°

the word
that made him available
is not available
to him

is this the man
who opted for a teaspoon
over a lifeboat
in open ocean
because seahorses
needed to drown
in his mouth

how salt is imagined
is how water concludes every violence
with a necessary beginning

233°

the snake
offers us each
one fang

in turn
we offer the snake
twelve bushels of veins
/fresh cut/

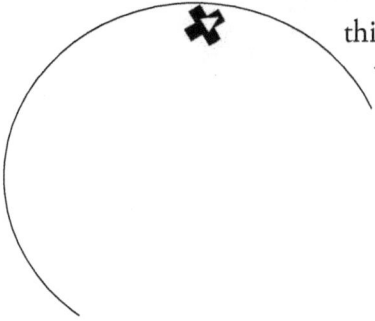

this is the town
where sleep lugs
deflated eyeballs in a bag
selling them /door to door/

156°

keys asleep under our skin
that would turn these locks
        into milk we could drink
            at the entrance
            to another life

255°

looking over you
at eight days old
i knew we were the same age

with the same blade
the circumcision
was meant to continue
around my neck

purity astounds the cut

194°

i spill seven poems from an inkwell

before they can dry
they all get up off the paper
inside the bodies of seven girls
who look at me
as if i am their reflection
adolescent to a line
they will draw on themselves
→ as women

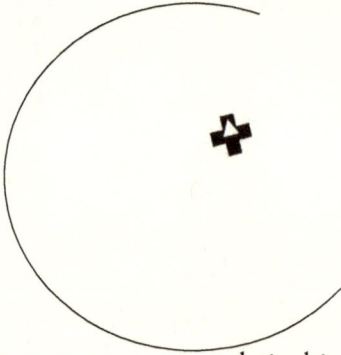

all have your face
but covet different expressions
portraits caught in encaustic
where they put their hands
between the other's legs
and promise to feel a penis
that isn't there

their thirst is such
that they drink a father's words
through pinholes
in the eyelids of his son

348°

our lips dam the silence

others will drown
if we open our mouths

if we open our mouths
we will save each other

346°

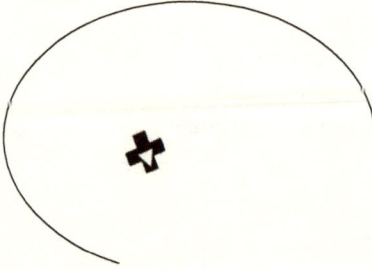

they told us about a heart
impregnated
with a suitcaseful of thermometers

zero takes its temperature
inside its own circle

347°

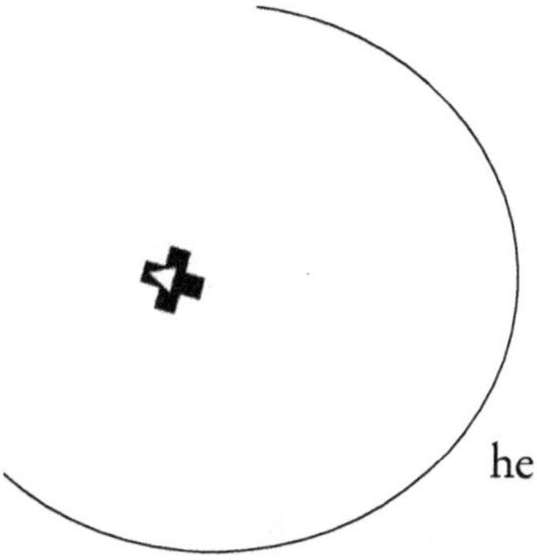

i throw a stone
to forget what a stone is

he lets he

i am i
among you

201°

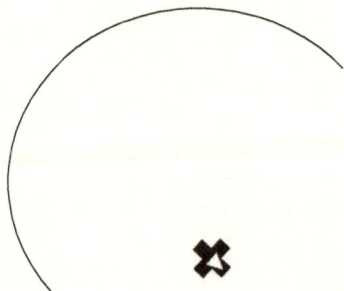

the one remark
that anchors the universe
to all it attracts
to all else unmentioned
in its biography of chaos

the traction
of a hidden planet
in the lines on your hand

53°

finding the knife
in its most worthy extension

my right ear
points to this poem ←

vocal drips on a leaf

299°

counsel the abstract
in this elastic room
where the same heads
instruct themselves in the art
of scissiparity

counsel the abstract
within the remains of this room
where i fire single photons
through two slits
to form three lines
on your chest
knowing you understand
the middle line
is your father

by (this) time ←
you are unable to read (this)
our bodies now suspended
in unidentified space
as a pure vertical mechanism
head crowns connected
upright/inverted
our flesh preserved
me spinning one way
you the other
as we orbit
around the only word
i never wrote

Notes

how to spear sleep is based on Paul Celan's fear that poetry would demand he re/enact 'Abraham's sacrifice' with his son Eric as the intended victim. This idea was reported by André du Bouchet. It is based on conversations between du Bouchet and Celan's wife Gisèle Celan-Lestrange and Eric Celan. It is also alluded to in correspondence between Paul Celan and his wife.

See *Letter #10* (14 January 1970), Paul Celan *Selections*, edited Pierre Joris (Los Angeles: University of California Press, 2005)

67° (p.32)
See Friedrich Dürrenmatt *On Paul Celan at Neuchâtel*, (*Selections*, edited Joris). Dürrenmatt recounts a pleasant afternoon spent playing table tennis with Celan. The closing line is from Dürrenmatt's essay.

155° (p.56)

The capitals refer to Paul Celan's original name Paul Antschel.

83° (p.69)
A reading of the photo Paul Celan and his son at their summer home, August 1958, (*Selections*, edited Joris).

This sequence was written 10.07–08.08.2012, apart from 220° (written 27.07.2011).

There is a system to the numbered titles and to the simple graphics imposed on each poem. The titles in degrees signify the orbit or oscillation around the original idea. The number of words within each poem were added together in continuously accruing cycles between 0 and 360 degrees. The sums were calculated in the order in which the poems were written. The set of answers was then redistributed by chance to each poem in the eventual order in which the book is now organised. The cross / triangle symbol (or CARD*) in each poem is at the rotated angle of each poem's original number.

* CARD = Celan Axial Rotational Device

Acknowledgements

The works in this collection were written in South East Queensland. I acknowledge the traditional custodians of that land and pay my respects to Elders past, present and emerging.

Thank you to Felicity Plunkett for the supply of portable horizons in her pocket and for her capacity to view the 'dark ocean of dark eyes'.

For their encouragement with this work thank you to Elisa Biagini, Pascalle Burton, Margie Cronin, Eve Fraser and Tiffany Johnson.

Shepherdson thanks to Ariel, Isaak and Luke.

Thank you to Tony Frazer and the being that is Shearsman for support and interest over many years.

1	16	39	55
2	39	348	64
3	58	248	12
4	98	300	8
5	126	39	7
6	155	7	24
7	218	126	54
8	270	349	5
9	288	347	66
10	315	113	31
11	349	177	44
12	4	277	10
13	67	55	17
14	83	131	2
15	95	88	58
16	113	325	37
17	131	16	49
18	156	264	34
19	177	53	68
20	194	98	50
21	230	69	43
22	255	71	35
23	299	33	3
24	338	225	52
25	7	211	47
26	33	300	51
27	69	233	60
28	95	138	39
29	126	255	62
30	155	253	1
31	233	122	13
32	253	91	36
33	347	194	63
34	59	16	33
35	122	248	32

36	150	270	4
37	183	151	40
38	201	12	16
39	211	359	23
40	225	230	11
41	248	4	42
42	264	220	30
43	281	150	21
44	302	156	61
45	359	281	6
46	39	95	41
47	55	141	15
48	71	315	20
49	88	155	29
50	106	338	57
51	138	201	67
52	158	346	65
53	220	20	27
54	248	59	53
55	277	95	18
56	300	126	28
57	348	58	59
58	12	288	26
59	53	218	25
60	67	44	46
61	91	158	38
62	151	83	56
63	300	67	22
64	346	155	45
65	20	302	19
66	325	106	48
67	16	67	9
68	44	183	14
69	141	299	69